Roundy & Friends
Book Nine

Andres Varela

Illustrations and Graphic Design by Carlos F. González
Co-Producer Germán Hernández
Third Edition
© 2019 Soccertowns® LLC

Previously...

The group has travelled along the highways from Texas all the way to Kansas City, Chicago, Columbus, Washington, New York and Massachusetts, and now they're heading across the US Border to Canada. They're going North on I-89. Their first destination is Montreal in the Province of Quebec.

A Province and a Territory in Canada are comparable to a State in the United States. There are 10 Provinces in the country as well as 3 Territories.

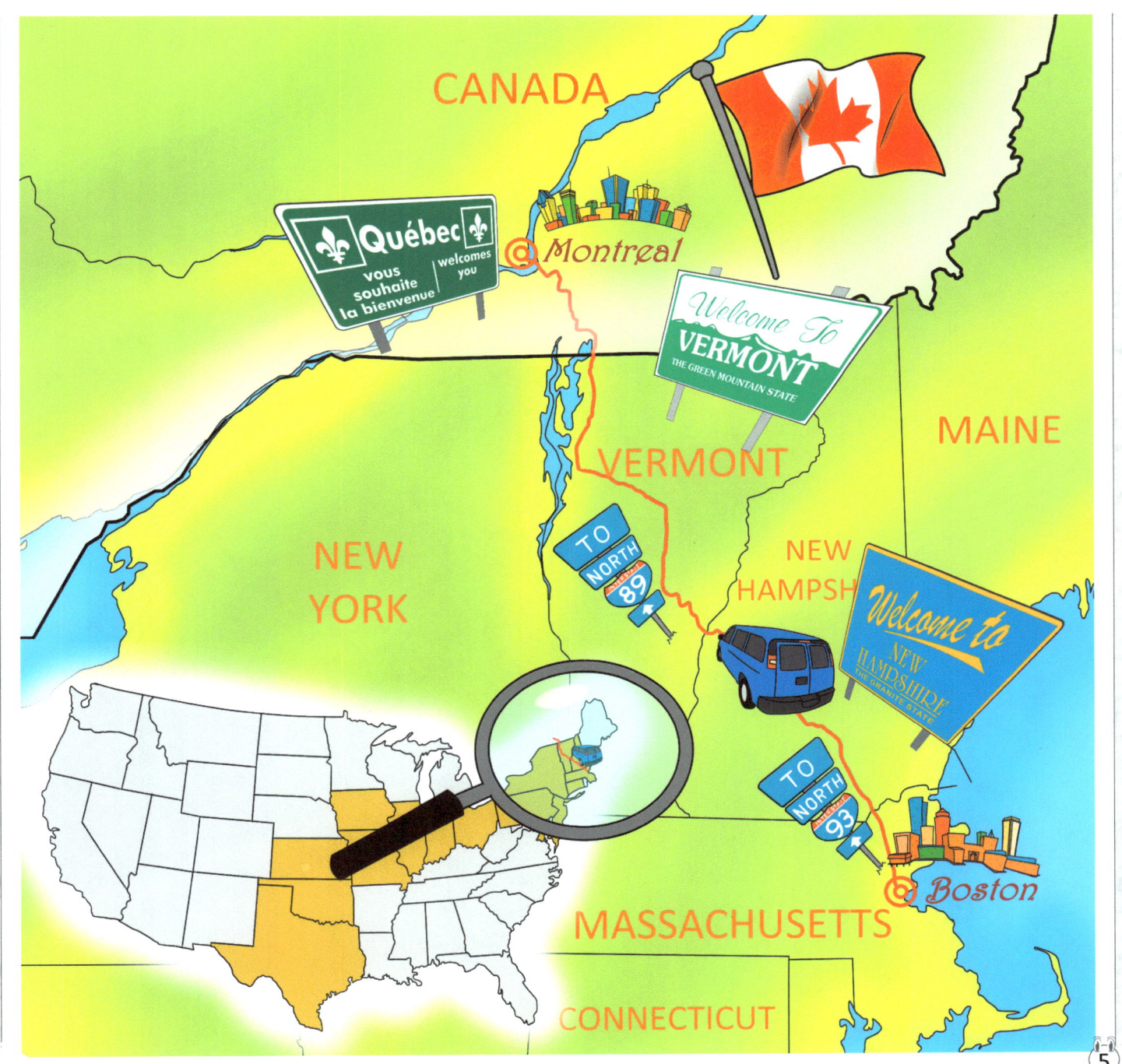

They arrive at the Swanton, Vermont border crossing, where they have to drive through customs and immigration to enter Canada.
Customs and immigration is where people coming to a new country have to show their passport, register and declare the stuff they have with them.

With 8 Canadian Provinces and 13 US States on each side, the border between the United States (US) and Canada is the longest international border in the world at 5,525 miles (8,891 Km).

Close to the customs and immigration booths, video cameras record all traffic crossing the border. The cameras also take pictures of car license plates, which are checked in a computer while people talk to the immigration officer.

It is estimated that more than 300,000 people cross the border everyday.

Once they cross, they enter Saint-Armond, Quebec and continue on to Montreal.
Montreal is the second most populated city in Canada. Over 4.6 million people live in the metropolitan area.
It is also a very diverse city with more than half of its people speaking both English and French. It is the second largest French speaking city in the World after Paris. Marie and Danielle speak French, which will help the rest of the team talk to the local people.
In 1976 Montreal hosted the 21st Summer Olympics.

The city built the Olympic Village, including the Olympic Stadium for this event.
The Olympic Stadium tower is a beautiful structure that holds the cables for the retractable roof of the stadium.

The stadium is now used for many sports, including baseball and football games. It is even used for big soccer games when needed because it can hold so many people.

Teo remembers the inauguration ceremony of the Olympics in 1976. It was a beautiful show!

The rest of the team runs all over the stadium after getting a special permit allowing them to learn about its history for a couple hours.

They decide to race 100 meters on the Olympic track. Roundy wins, rolling to victory, due to his body shape allowing him to go faster than the others! Teo tells the team "Speed is also important in the game of soccer, to score goals or to defend against faster opponents. We have to keep practicing our speed!"

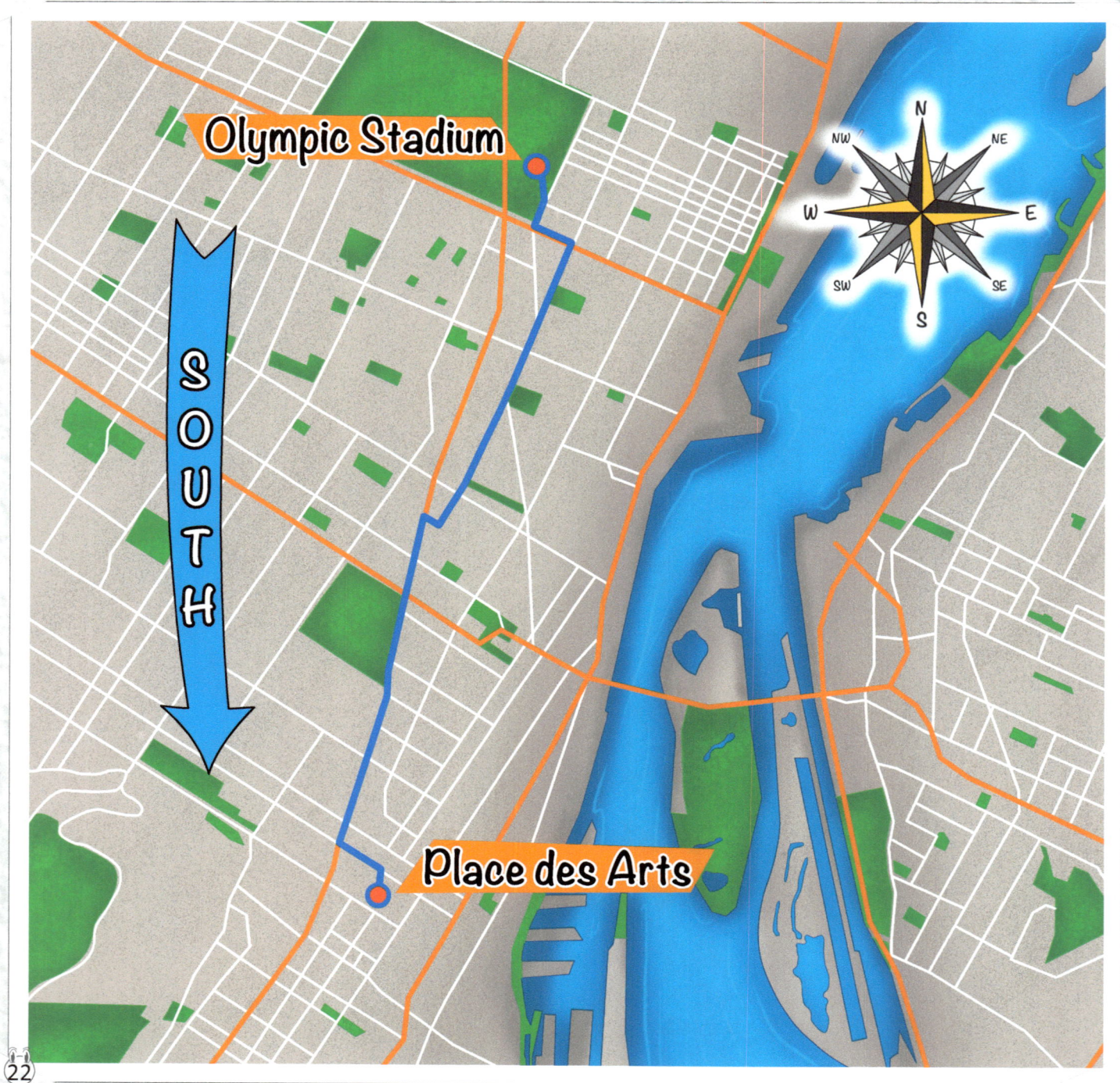

After a fun time at the stadium, the team heads south towards Place de Arts, a performing arts center and the largest artistic and cultural complex in Montreal.

Created in 1963, it has 6 different theaters of various sizes. Roundy enjoys the variety of things to see and listen to. He doesn't remember ever being to a concert.

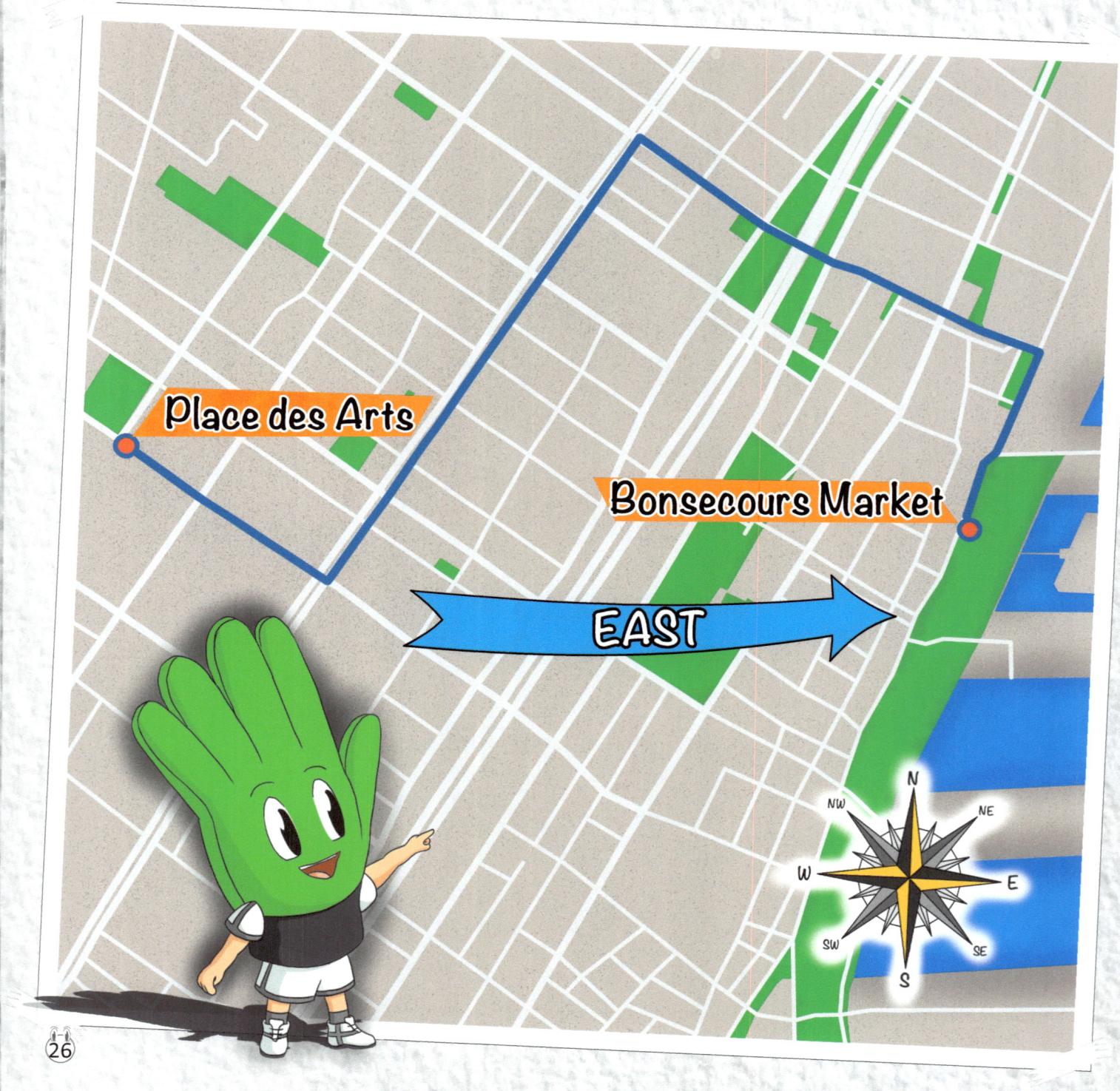

After Place des Arts, they head East to Bonsecours Market, the largest public market in the Montreal area for over 100 years.

They learn the first building was completed in 1847.

Ben says "Wow, that was a very long time ago."

Bonsecours Market

Outside Bonsecours Market, the team walks along the pleasant pathways, getting to enjoy a very nice afternoon outdoors.

Jersey says, "look at that big bridge."

Danielle responds, "that is the Jacques Cartier Bridge, it was built in 1930."

"It's such a beautiful day" said Emma, "let's go to the park to have a picnic." They decide to go to a park for a picnic. They agree on going to Beaver Lake and drive Southwest.

They all reflect about their trip to Montreal while having their picnic. It was very interesting because it was so different than cities in the United States.

Come back and read the next story, we're heading to Toronto!......

www.ingramcontent.com/pod-product-compliance
Lightning Source LLC
Chambersburg PA
CBHW041501220426
43661CB00016B/1213